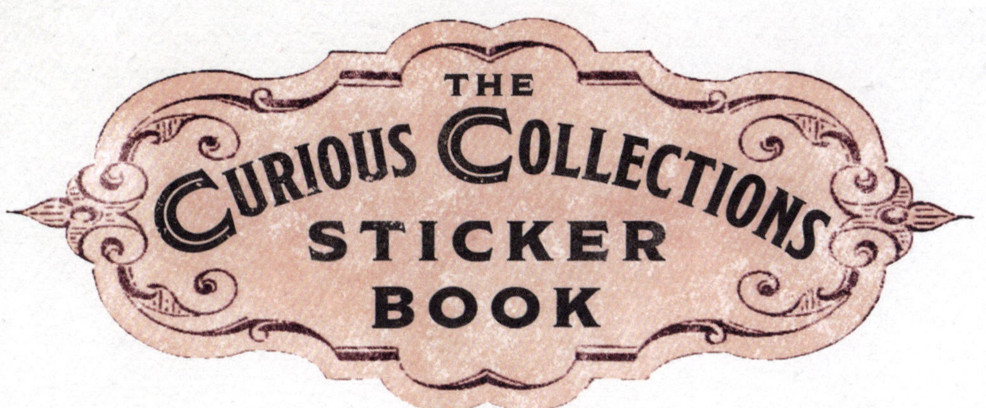

Skittledog

LOVE BIRDS
SAFETY MATCHES
50's PRICE 13 PS.
RIMCO
CHOKKAN MATCH INDUSTRIES.
KAMUTHI.

MADE IN JAPAN
中國利興公司

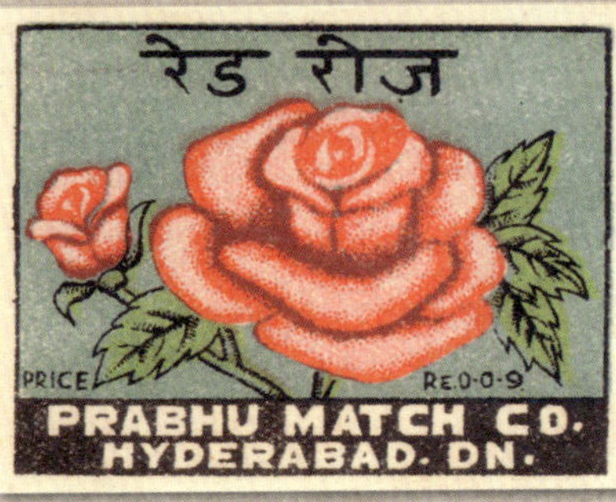
रेड रोज़
PRICE
RE.0-0-9
PRABHU MATCH CO.
HYDERABAD. DN.

TRADE MARK
MADE IN JAPAN
HOP CHONG
錦章洋行

IMPREGNATED
CUPPLES
RHINO
SAFETY MATCHES
MADE IN SWEDEN

கடல் கன்னி
PRICE RE.0-0-6.
THE ARUMUGAM MATCH INDUSTRIES

SWEETY
WAX 50's
30 Ps.
THIRUMALAI MATCH INDUSTRIES.
SIPPIPARAI.

Suyodhana
50's SAFETY MATCHES
PRICE 13 Ps.
KOHINOOR MATCH INDUSTRIES
TADPATRI.

ALMACEN "EL GATO"
MATCHES MADE IN SWEDEN
TON LEY LON Cº GUATEMALA

火
虎
柴
標

IMPREGNATED
SAFETY MATCHES
MADE IN FINLAND
CARMEN

LOVE
PRICE Re0-06.
SAFETY MATCHES
SRI ANDAL MATCH FACTORY
KOVILPATTI.

播磨燐寸株式會社
鶴
盃
精撰優等品

BIGBOSS
SAFETY MATCHES
ANESBSSK, KONGORPILLY, P.O

MADE IN SWEDEN
SAFETY MATCHES
AVERAGE COUNT 60 MATCHES

PRICE RE.0.06.
NARAHARIPOORNENDRA
MATCH WORKS ONGOLE

"FISH"
TRADE
MARK
REGISTERED
SAFETY MATCHES

品
優
特撰
マッチ
質
良
中部燐寸會社謹製

SAFETY
MATCHES
MADE
IN SWEDEN

SAFETY MATCHES
PING
PONG
TOHOKU MATCH CO.

SINDHU
RAJALAKSHMI MATCH FACTORY.
V. SALVARPATTI. (VIA) SIVAKASI.

SHIVAJI
SAFETY MATCHES
SOUNDRAPANDIAN MATCH WORKS

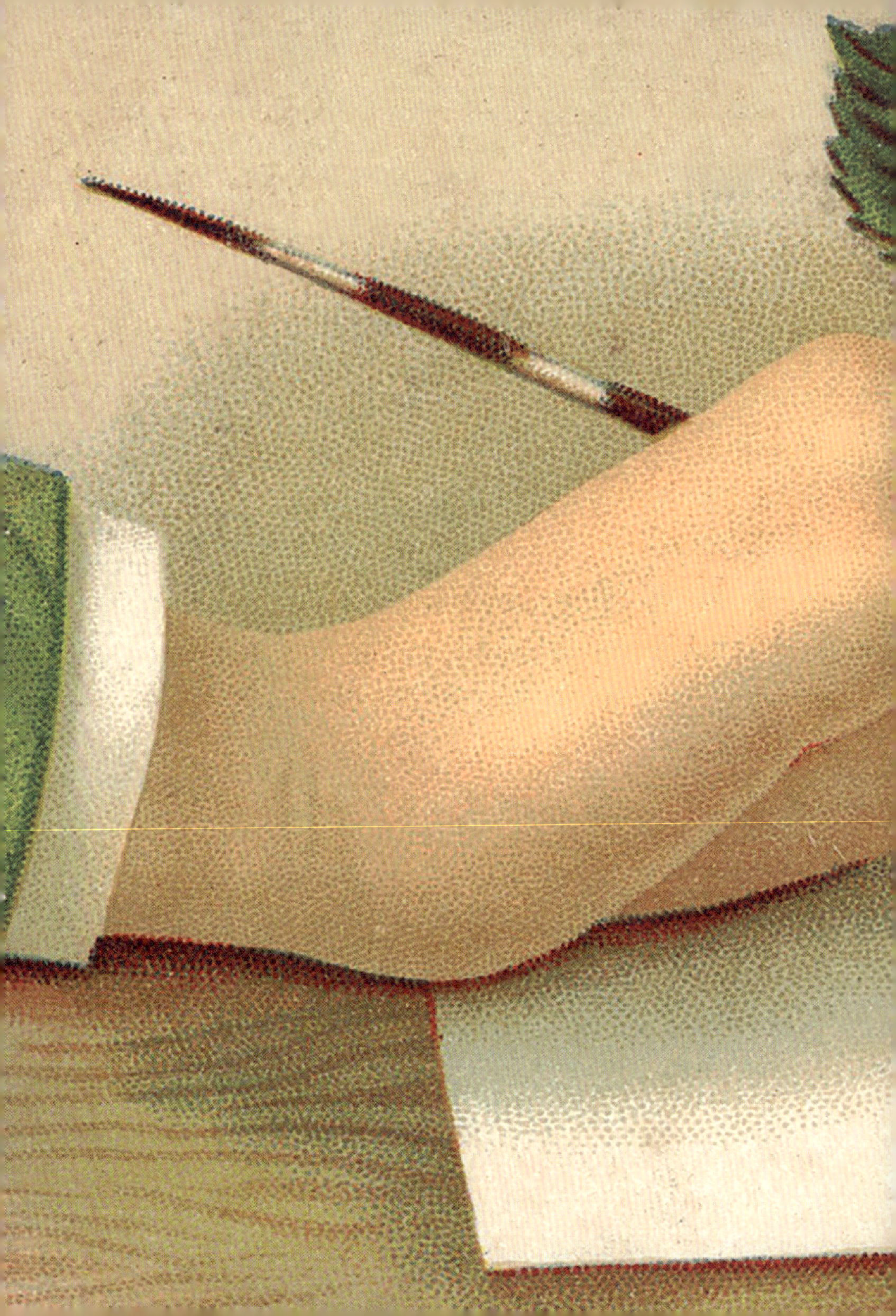

Compliments of the
Domestic S.M.

Devotion.
A token of friendship.
FORGET ME NOT

MY HEART IS THINE
In fond remembrance
Keep me in thy Memory
MAY BLOOM
VIOLET BLOOM

LA VIE

RISIENNE

SIGAUT
PARIS
15 MÉDAILLES D'OR
15 DIPLÔMES D'HON.
GRAND PRIX LONDRES 1908

CONFITURERIE JULIEN DAMOY
MARQUE
DÉPOSÉE
PARIS

LE BON CAMEMBERT
FABRIQUÉ A LA LAITERIE COOP. DE REIGNAC
40%

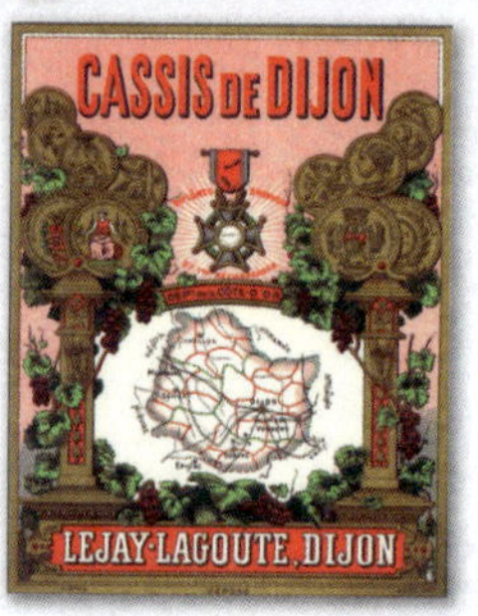
CASSIS DE DIJON
LEJAY-LAGOUTE, DIJON

SIROP
DE
MENTHE
PUR
SUCRE

HUILE D'OLIVE
SUBLIME
clarifiée double
LAURENT FRERES
MARSEILLE.

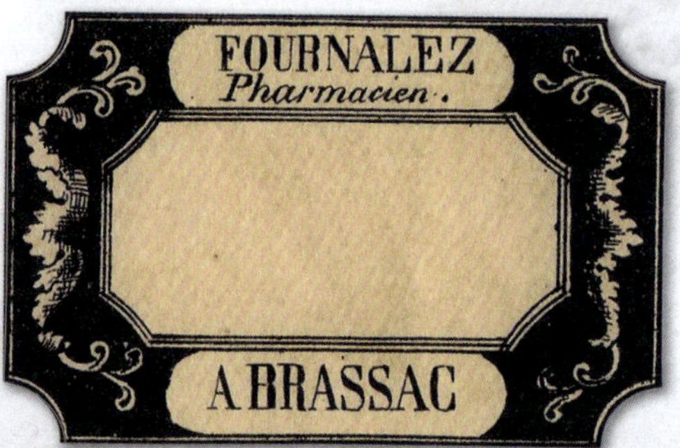
FOURNALEZ
Pharmacien.
A BRASSAC

PARFUMERIE
AU PRINCIPE
DES FLEURS
ESSENCE CONCENTRÉE
A LA GIROFLÉE BLANCHE
PRÉPARÉE
PAR
J. GIRAUD FILS
Grasse, Paris

Eau
DE
Cologne

PARIS

NO.
LA FAVORITE
ONE
DOZ

CERISES
1ER CHOIX

SIROP DE
GRENADINE
PUR
SUCRE

SIROP DE
GRENADINE
PUR SUCRE
Nº530

ESSENCE CONCENTRÉE
HÉLIOTROPE BLANC
JN GIRAUD FILS
Parfumeur
GRASSE-PARIS

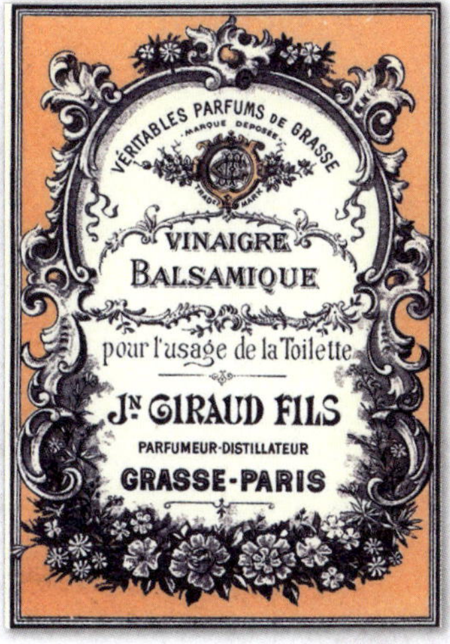
VÉRITABLES PARFUMS DE GRASSE
VINAIGRE
BALSAMIQUE
pour l'usage de la Toilette
JN GIRAUD FILS
PARFUMEUR-DISTILLATEUR
GRASSE-PARIS

LE MEILLEUR
ROUGE SUPÉRIEUR
11º

VÉRITABLES PARFUMS AUX FLEURS
ESSENCE CONCENTRÉE
ROSE DE PROVENCE
JN GIRAUD FILS
PARFUMEUR
GRASSE
PARIS

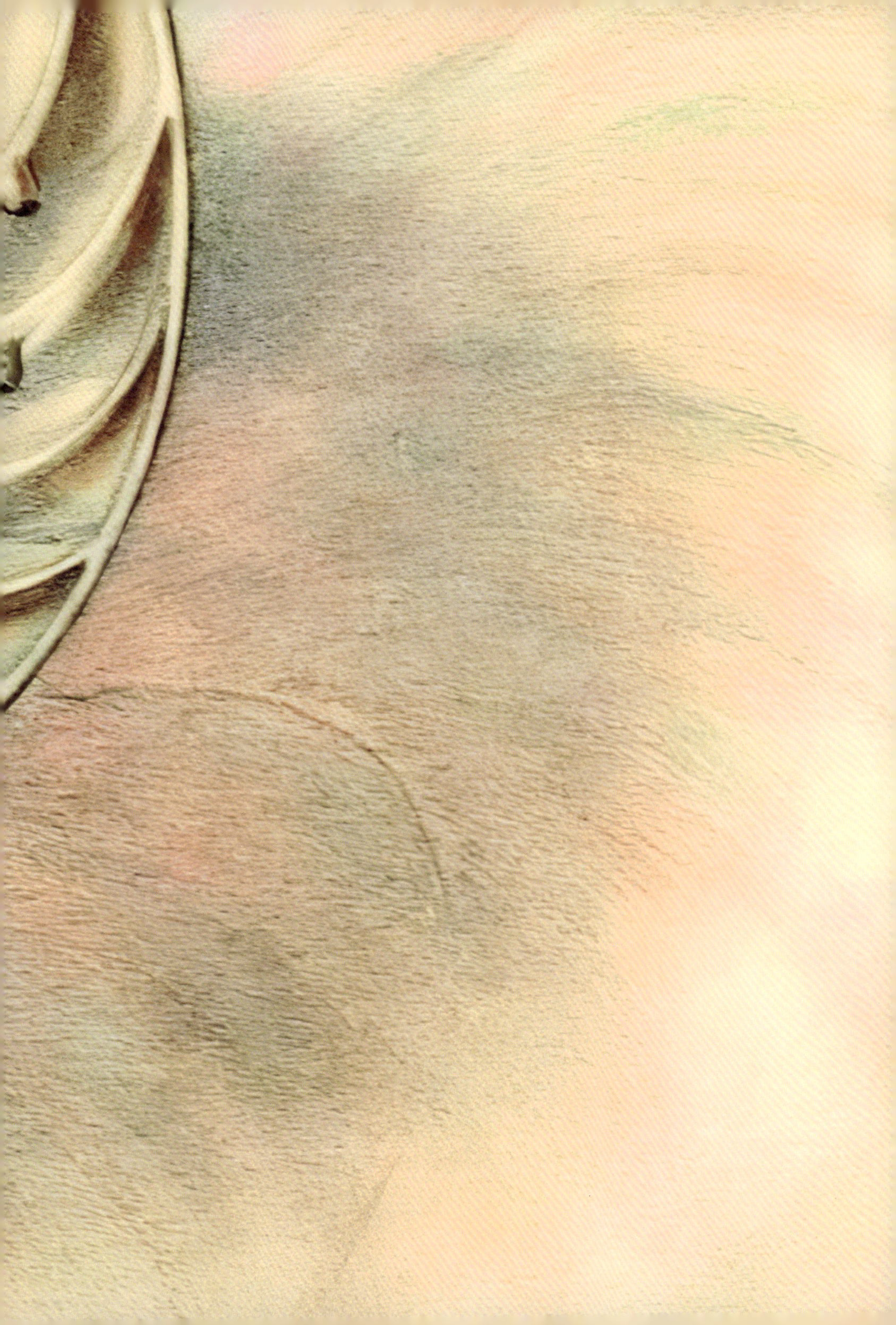

A
B
C
D
E
F
G
H
I
K
L
M
N
O
P

A
B
C
D
E
F
G
L
I
K
H
M
N
O
P
Q
R

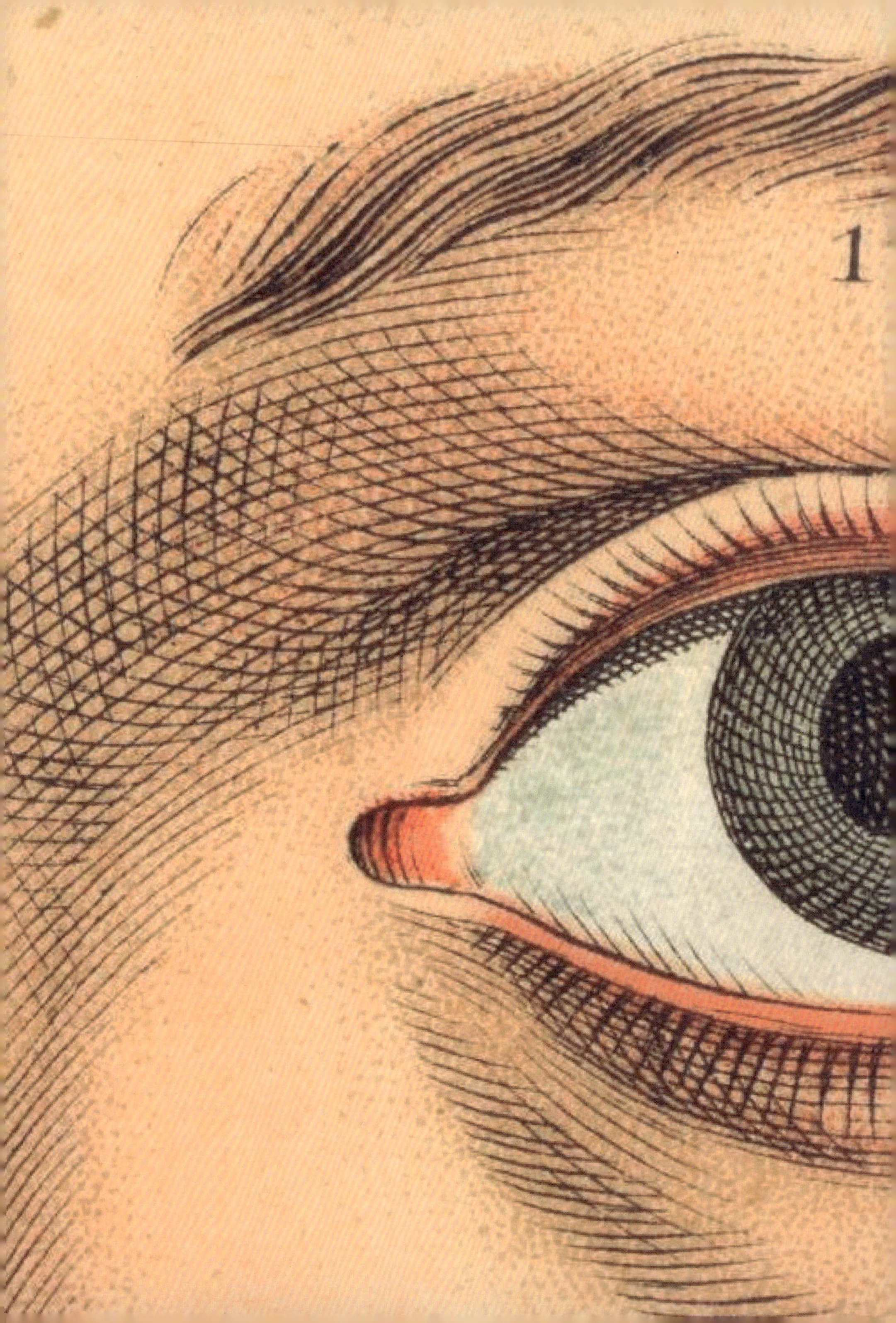
1

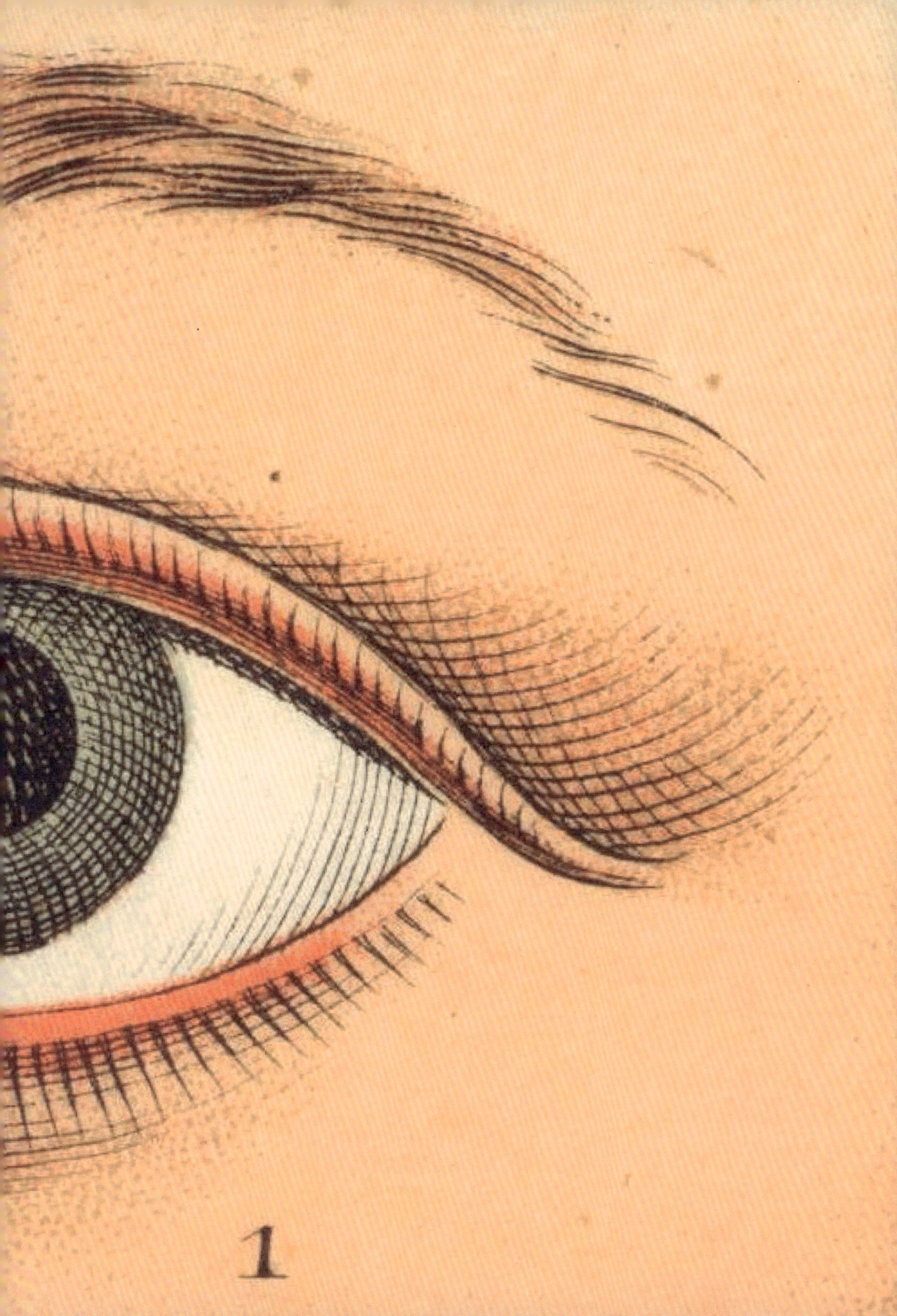
1

Send your address and get more wonders for 25 cts. than $10 will buy at home.
MODEST & ATTRACTIVE PHOTOGRAPHS
MOUNTED TO SUIT LADIES OR GNTS
OUR SAN.Y COM.N CURIOSITY
ADMITS
PACKAGES CONTAIN UPWARDS OF ONE HUNDRED NEW AND BEAUTIFUL SPECIMENS ALL FOR 25 CENTS
BEAUTIFUL BOOK MARKS

All goods sent by return mail by M. Westbrook & Co., No. 12 9th Street, N.Y.
SOLDIERS
and AGENTS should send for
CERTIFICATES & CATALOGUES
UNITED
TAKE TIME by the FORELOCK
PREPARE TO DOUBLE their MONEY ON PAY DAY

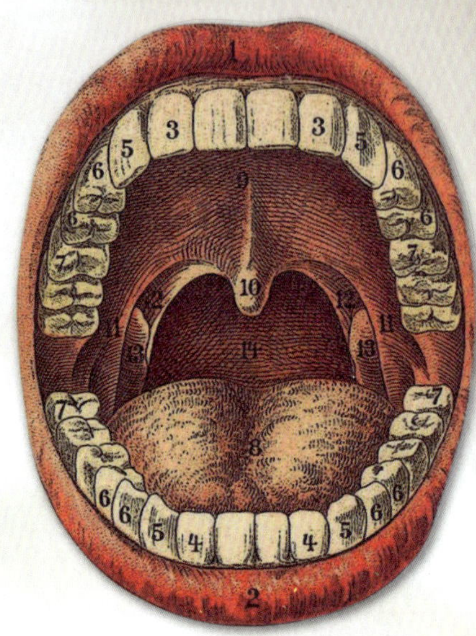

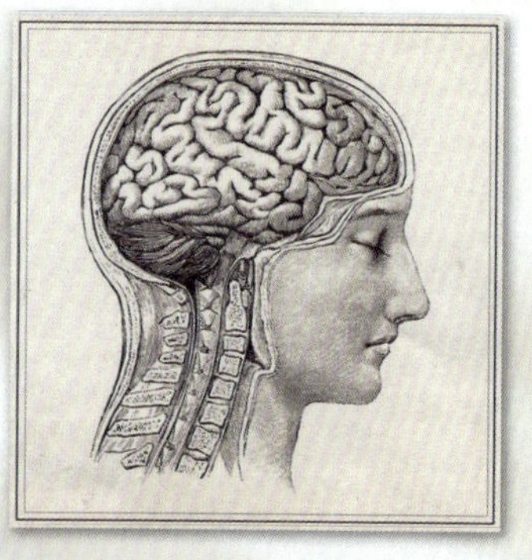

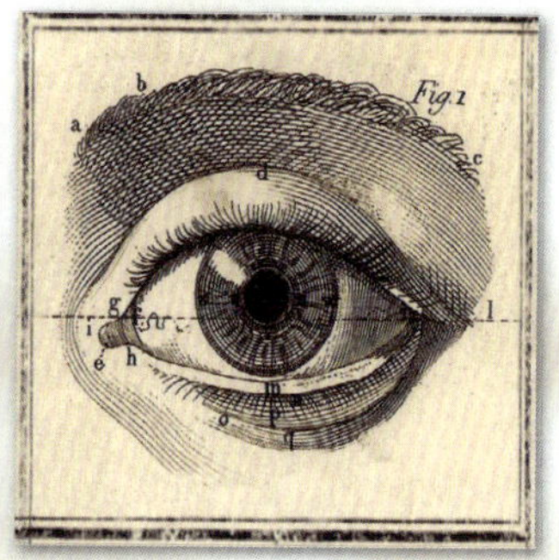
Fig. 1

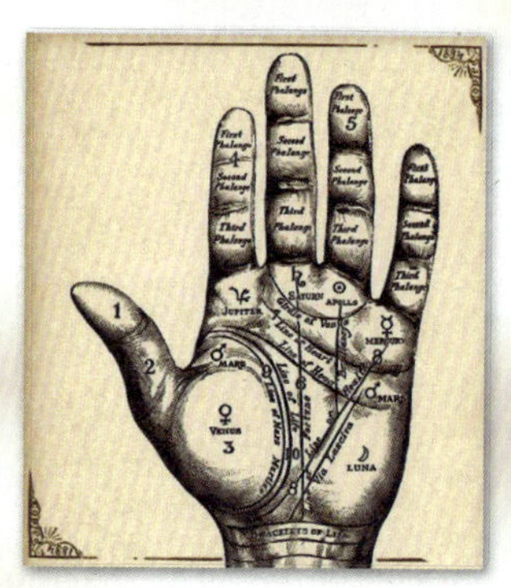
VENUS
LUNA

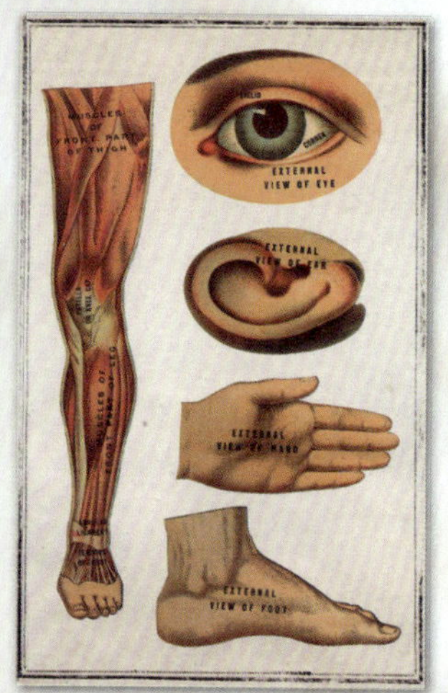
EXTERNAL VIEW OF EYE
EXTERNAL VIEW OF EAR
EXTERNAL VIEW OF HAND
EXTERNAL VIEW OF FOOT

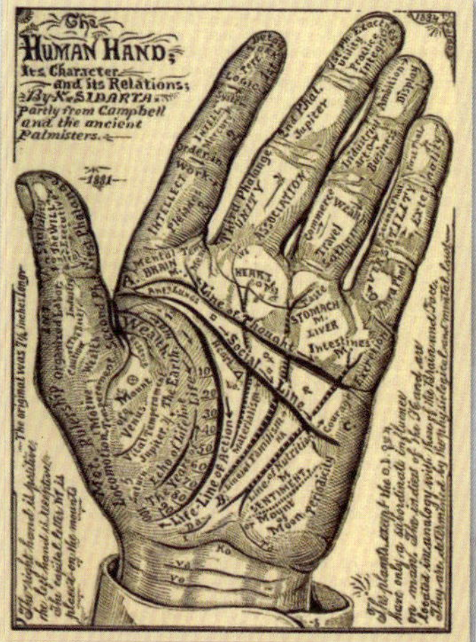
The HUMAN HAND,
Its Character and its Relations;
By K. SIDARTA;
Partly from Campbell and the ancient Palmisters.

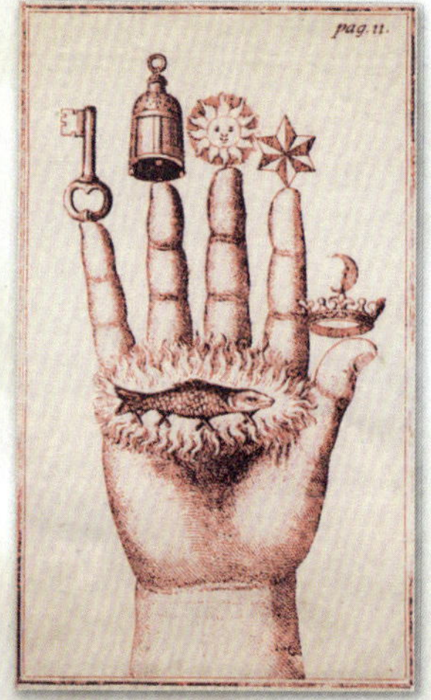
pag. 11.

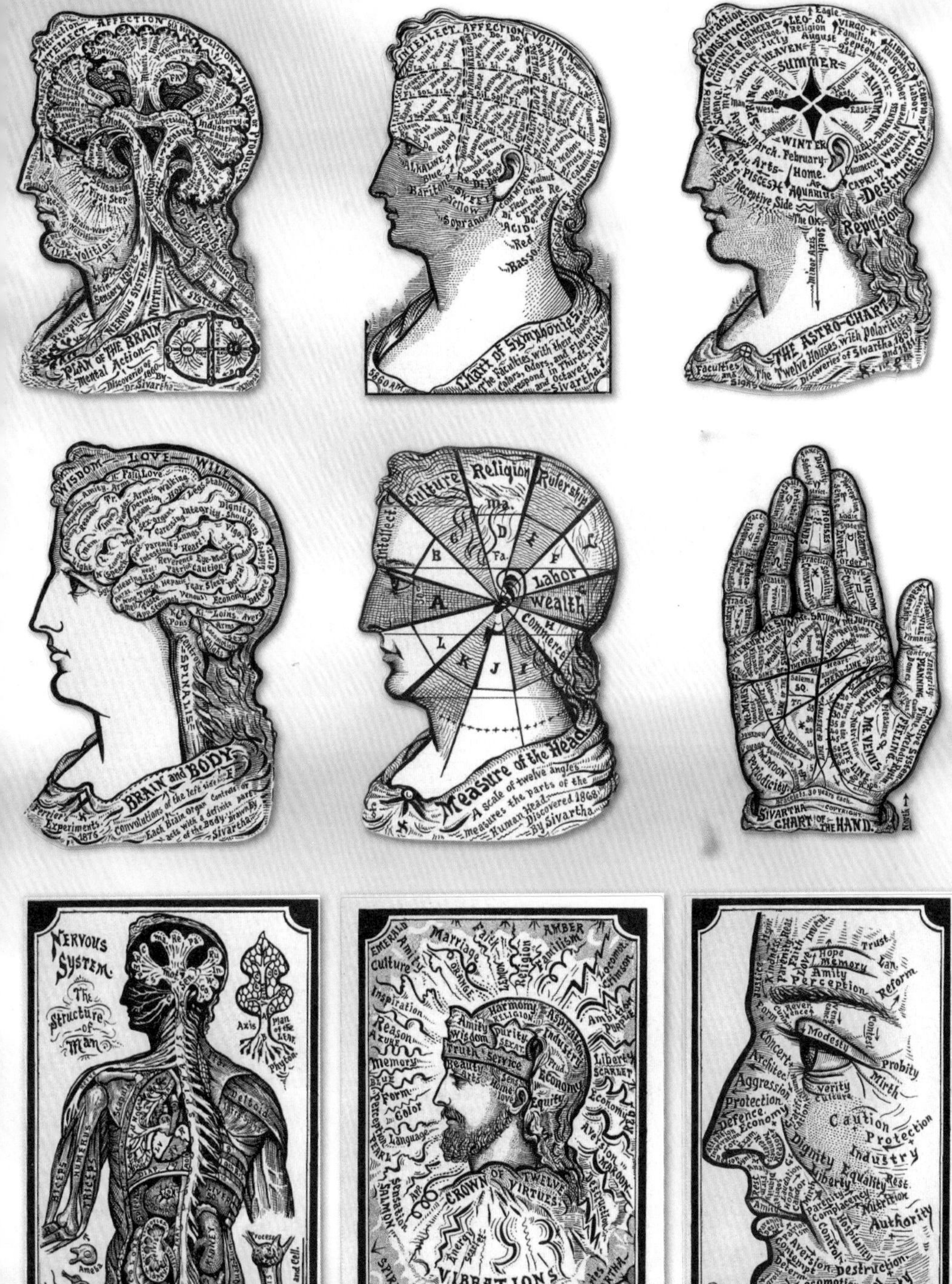

Plan of the Brain
Mental Action
Discoveries of 1860 By Dr. Sivartha
Chart of Symphonies
The Faculties with their Tones, Colors, Odors, and Flavors, Correspond in Thirds, Fifths and Octaves.
Sivartha
The Astro-Chart
The Twelve Houses, with Polarities
Discoveries of Sivartha 1859 and 1884
Summer
Winter
Brain and Body
Convolutions of the left side
Each Brain Organ Controls or acts with a definite part of the Body. Drawn By Sivartha
Ferrier's Experiments 1876
Wisdom
Love
Will
Measure of the Head
A scale of twelve angles measures the parts of the Human Head. Discovered 1868. By Sivartha.
Culture
Religion
Rulership
Intellect
Labor
Wealth
Commerce
Sivartha
Chart of the Hand
Nervous System
The Structure of Man
Crown of Twelve Virtues
Vibrations
Spiritual Light
Discoveries By Sivartha 1860
Aurosphere
A Chart of the Face
By Sivartha

PROTOGONIUS FABIUS.

THE COMMON TIGER MOTH.

ARGGANIS PANDOSA
(Under side).

THE DEATHS' HEAD MOTH.
(Acherontia atlopos).

EVENUS REGALIS.

CETHOSIA MAHRATTA.

HIPOCRITA JACOBŒÆ
THE CINNABAR MOTH.

ILIADES AGENOR.

THE PAINTED LADY. NANESSA CARDUI.

ERATINA
LEPTOCIRCATA.

MORPHO ADONIS.

METAMORPHA DIDO. (Under side).

MELITÆA CINXIA
THE GLANVILLE FRITILLARY.

EUCHROMIA POLYMENA.

MINIODES DISCOLOR.

CHRYSIRIDIA MADAGASCARIENSIS.

ANTEROS ACHAEUS.

THE SILVER STUDDED BLUE
(Plebeius Argus).

CALIGO ILIONEUS.

EUPTYCHIA
BRIXIUS.

ILIADES AGENOR.

THE PAINTED LADY. NANESSA CARDUI.

HELICOPIS ACIS.

HECTORIDES ASCANIUS.

THE LAPPET MOTH. GASTROPACHA QUERCIFOLIA

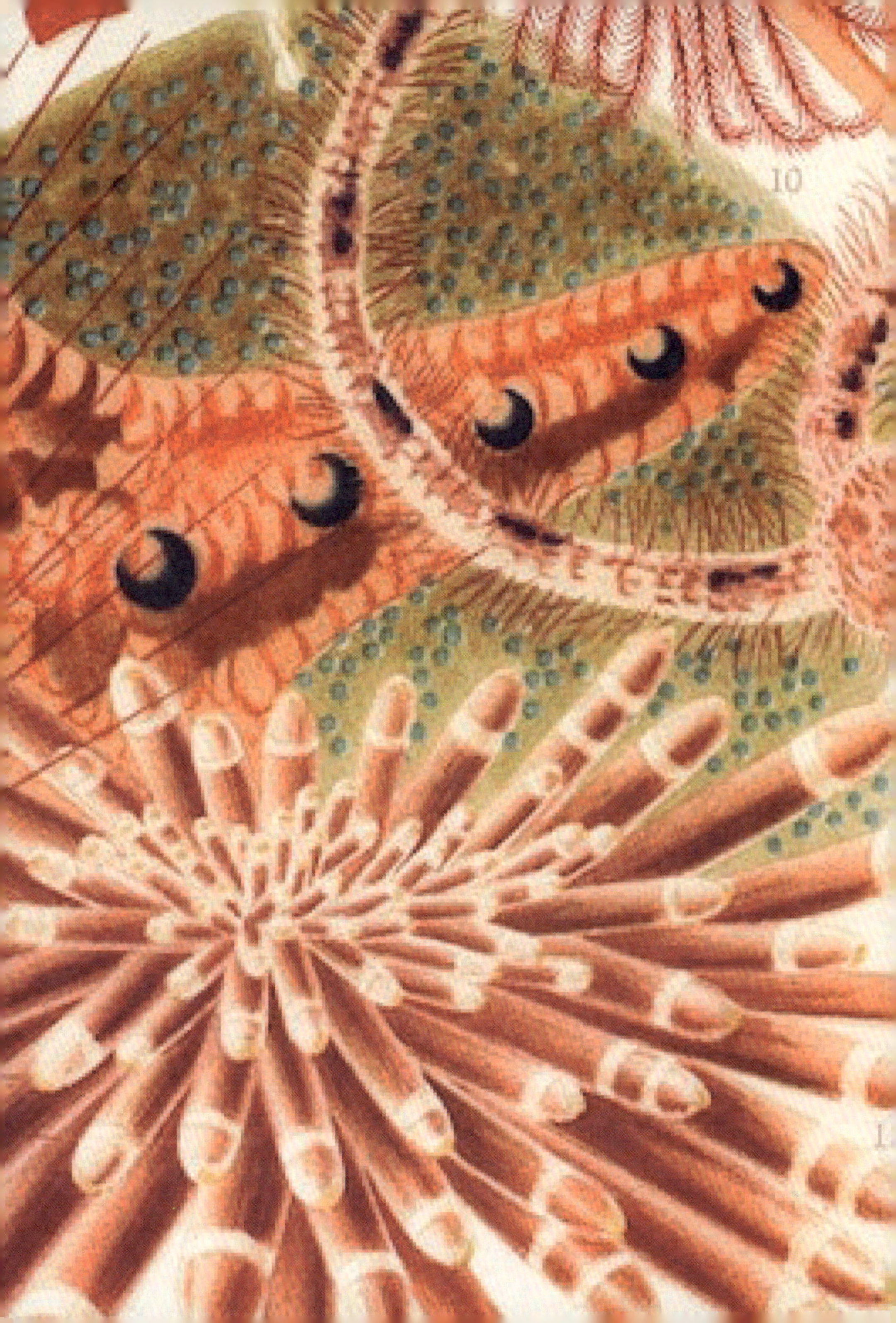
10

A
B

1. Albus	2. Griseus	3. Murinus	4. Ater	5. Niger
6. Fumosus	7. Avellaneus	8. Isabellinus	9. Umbrinus	10. Castaneus
11. Fuligineus	12. Atropurpureus	13. Purpureus	14. Ruber	15. Miniatus
16. Incarnatus	17. Roseus	18. Testaceus	19. Latericius	20. Badius
21. Aurantiacus	22. Luteus	23. Flavus	24. Citrinus	25. Sulphureus

26. Stramineus	27. Cremeus	28. Ochroleucus	29. Ochraceus	30. Melleus
31. Ferrugineus	32. Fulvus	33. Flavo-virens	34. Atro-virens	35. Viridis
36. Prasinus	37. Aerugineus	38. Glaucus	39. Olivaceus	40. Atro-cyaneus
41. Cyaneus	42. Cæruleus	43. Cæsius	44. Plumbeus	45. Ardesiacus
46. Atro-violaceus	47. Violaceus	48. Lilacinus	49. Lividus	50. Vinosus

35
BANI
OMINA
AIDA TASGIAN-CONSTANTINESCU

POSTA
Ardei iute
R P R
1963

75
BANI

POSTA

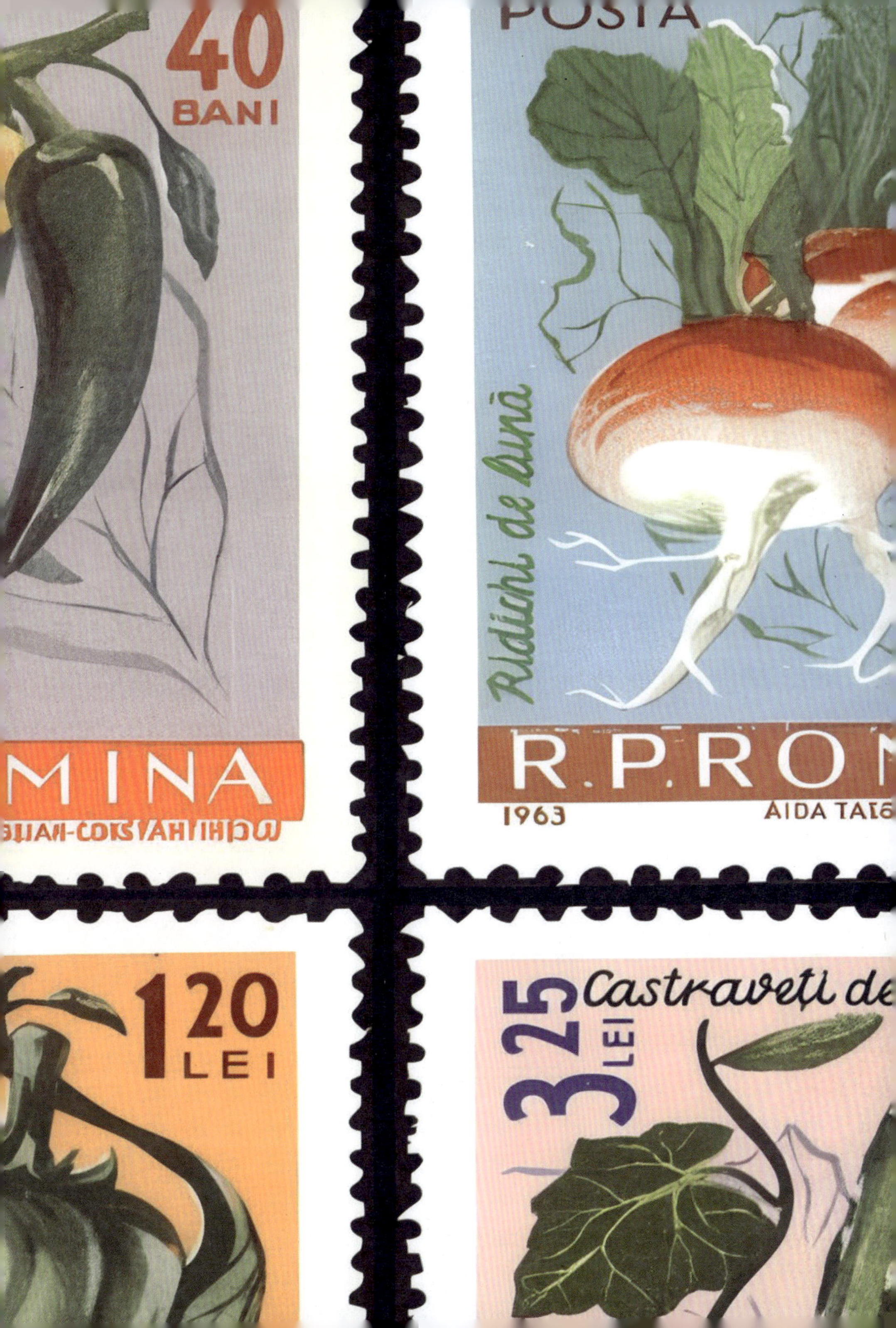

40
BANI

MINA

POSTA

Ridichi de lună

R.P.ROM

1963

AIDA TAT

ENERGY
DEVELOPMENT
USA 13c

МОРДОВСКАЯ АССР
ПОЧТА СССР
4 КОП.
1962 г. САРАНСК. ДОМ СОВЕТОВ

TEN 10 CENTS

OFFICIAL
3
STAMP
U S
THREE 3 CENTS

Strix uralensis Pallas
Huhurez mare
2010
MOLDOVA 1,20 L

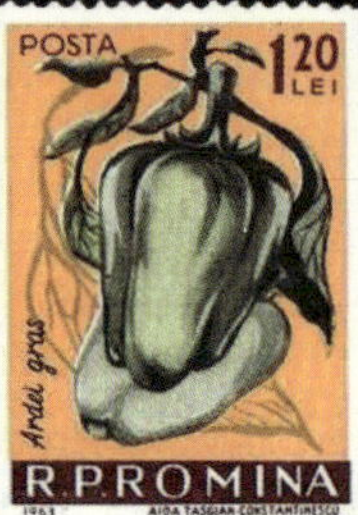
POSTA
1.20 LEI
Ardei gras
R.P.ROMINA
1963

POSTA
75 BANI
Vinete lungi
R.P.ROMINA
1963

POSTA
55 BANI
R.P.ROMINA
1963

13c USA
California
CALIFORNIA REPUBLIC
BICENTENNIAL ERA 1776-1976

POSTA
35 BANI
R.P.ROMINA
1963

RUSSIA · 2014 РОССИЯ
15 Р. Снежный барс – Uncia uncia

6c
UNITED STATES
Franklinia alatamaha

30 BANI
POSTA
R.P. ROMINA

RUSSIA · 2014 РОССИЯ
20 Р. Амурский тигр – Panthera tigris altaica

Dogface
USA 13c Colias eurydice

55 BANI
POSTA
R.P. ROMINA

RUSSIA · 2014 РОССИЯ
18 Р. Дальневосточный леопард – Panthera pardus orientalis

ПОЧТА СССР 1979
10 к
ПТИЦЫ-ЗАЩИТНИКИ ЛЕСА
Tyto alba
Сова сипуха

POSTAGE DUE
2
U S

POSTAGE DUE
30
U S

4к
АСТРАХАНСКИЙ ЗАПОВЕДНИК
СУЛТАНСКАЯ КУРИЦА
ПОЧТА СССР 1968

Иволга
Oriolus oriolus
ПТИЦЫ-ЗАЩИТНИКИ ЛЕСА
2к
ПОЧТА СССР 1979
Малый пестрый дятел
Dendrocopos minor
ПТИЦЫ-ЗАЩИТНИКИ ЛЕСА
3к
1979 ПОЧТА СССР

ПЕВЧИЕ ПТИЦЫ
РАСПИСНАЯ СИНИЧКА
6к
1981 ПОЧТА СССР

ПЕВЧИЕ ПТИЦЫ
РАЙСКАЯ МУХОЛОВКА
10к
1981 ПОЧТА СССР

ПЕВЧИЕ ПТИЦЫ
15к
1981 ПОЧТА СССР

БЪЛГАРСКА ПОЩА
ПЕТЬ СТОТИН.
5

Hawaiian
Postage
13
13 Cents.

CONFEDERATE STATES
FIVE CENTS

JAMAICA
£1

TELEGRAPHS
£5
£5
FIVE POUNDS

POSTAGE
WESTERN
AUSTRALIA
TWO PENCE
UNITED STATES
8¢
WILDLIFE CONSERVATION

CIRCUS
5c
UNITED STATES

EMPIRE FRANC
POSTES

1869
1944
POSTAGE
3¢
UNITED STATES OF AMERICA

БЪЛГАРСКА ПОЩА
ДЕСЕТЬ СТОТИН.
10

NEW YORK WORLD'S FAIR 1964
1965
5¢

6¢
US
PLANT for more BEAUTIFUL STREETS

WILDLIFE CONSERVATION
8¢
UNITED STATES

OFFICIAL
3
STAMP
OFFICIAL
6
STAMP

PLANT for more BEAUTIFUL HIGHWAYS

6¢
UNITED STATES
Franklinia alatamaha

A
B
C
D
firſt finds the way.
form a great A.
By a bright thought.
To a B he is brought.
He's forc'd to ſtrain hard.
Leſt the C ſhould be marr'd.
Now a D he is fo
With his Noſe to the
K
L
M
looks wiſtly dry.
hile in form of an I.
Do but look and you'll ſay,
Here ſtruts Comical K.
L ſits him down eaſy.
And hopes for to pleaſe ye.
Hah! Hah! here co
To accompany th
S
T
V
ls an R to your view.
ch I hope ſatiſfies you.
Here he's twiſted & twin'd.
To make S to your mind.
T next does exhibit.
In form of a Gibbet.
V joins with the ro
In their humorous
The Comical HOTCH-POTCH, or th
Printed for & Sold by CARINGTON BOWLES.
Do but

E

ith the reſt he'll agree,
nd aſſiſt them with E.

F

From the Head to the Feet.
He's an F quite complete.

G

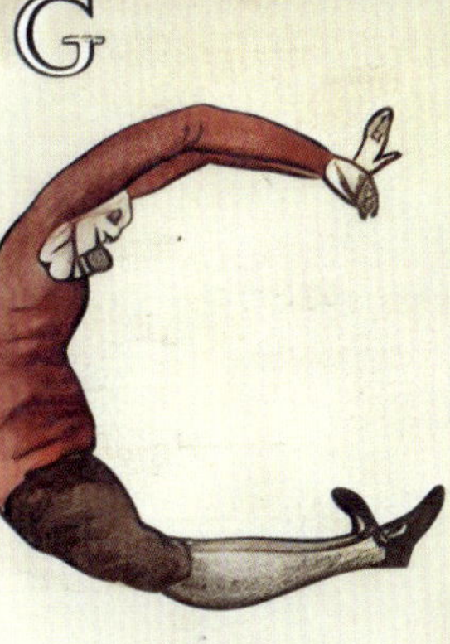

Look forward you'll ſee,
He's in form of a G.

H

With his Hands
An H does dec

N

ow N follows after.
o excite you to laughter.

O

Any body may know,
He's in form of an O.

P

Pray look at me,
In the form of a P.

Q

Any Shape I c
So a Q here I m

W

is ſtrange but moſt true.
hat I make W.

X

To pleaſe every Sex.
I am forming an X.

Y

With his Arms ſtill extended
For Y is intended.

Z

It will ſtick on my
If I can't make

PHABET turn'd POSTURE-MASTER

Comic Set —

at Nº69 in St Pauls Church Yard LONDON

日産農林工業株式會

製

つつじ
なのはな

もものはな

おもだか

あざみ

ばら

あじさい

まつばぼたん

のぎく

さくら

もものはな

ふじばかま
ふよう
すいれん
あさがお
りんどう
きょうちくとう
れんげ
うめ
さくらそう
さざんか
ぼたん

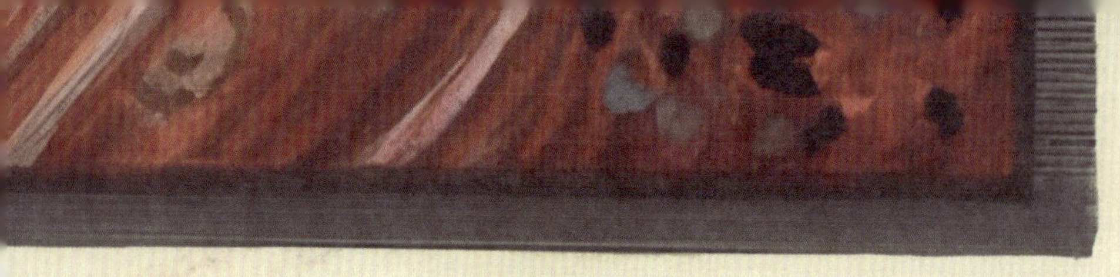

57.

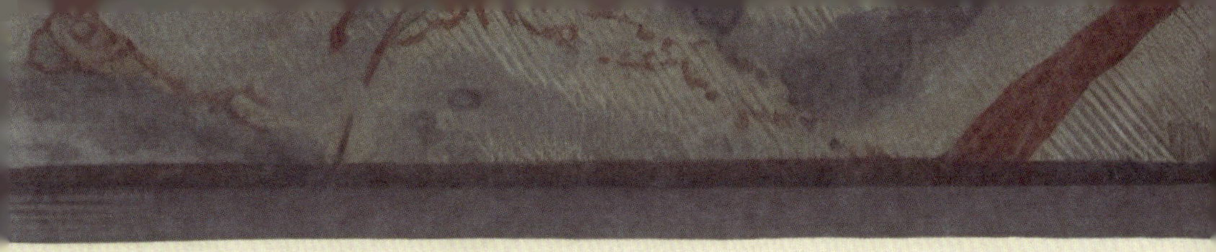

58.

1
2
3
4
5
6
7
8
9
10
11
12
13
14
15
16

16
28
13
12
15
17
18
10
30
32
19
20
21
7
3
9
36
31
2
1
14
22
5
30
3
23
24
25
21
4
39
6
36
11
27
8

HOTEL
Belvedere
SOLO SUSICE CSN 494705

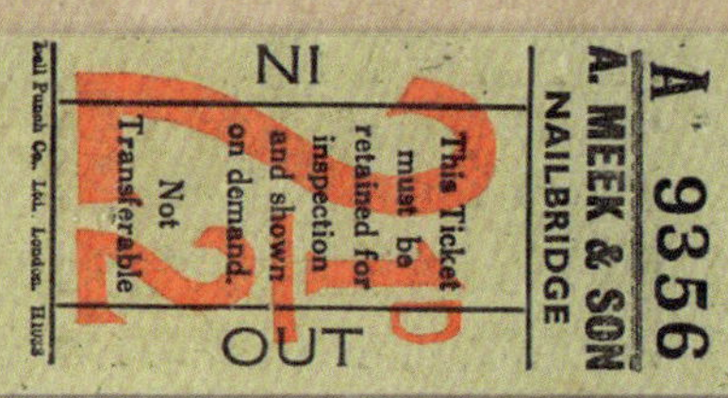
A 9356
A. MEEK & SON
NAILBRIDGE
This Ticket must be retained for inspection and shown on demand.
Not Transferable
IN
OUT

NORCANAIR
SASKATOON
19838

DELTA AIR LINES
YUL
Montreal, Quebec

D 9253
A. MEEK & SON
NAILBRIDGE
This Ticket must be retained for inspection and shown on demand.
Not Transferable
IN
OUT

C 1812
3d
q8462
2d

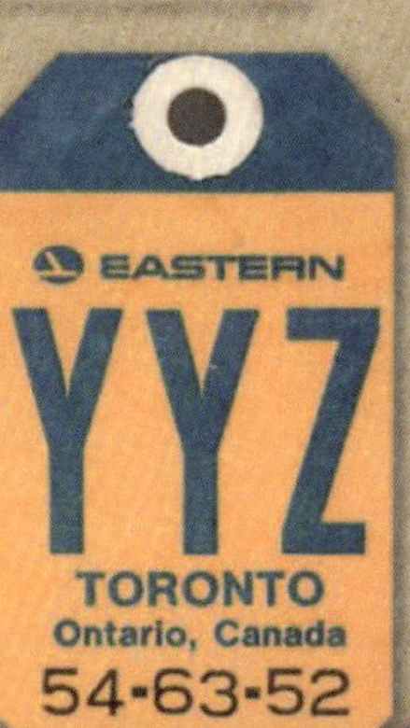
EASTERN
YYZ
TORONTO
Ontario, Canada
54-63-52

MEA
To Beirut
الى بيروت
BEY
Flight
ME 262

BI BI
NO. CHECKED PCS.
WEIGHT THIS PC.
TO MEXICO CITY
MEX
BRANIFF INTERNATIONAL
BN-71-02-60

Ac 5742
CHILDREN'S TICKET

TIME AIR
CALGARY ALTA
151761

LON
FLIGHT NUMBER
62
192246

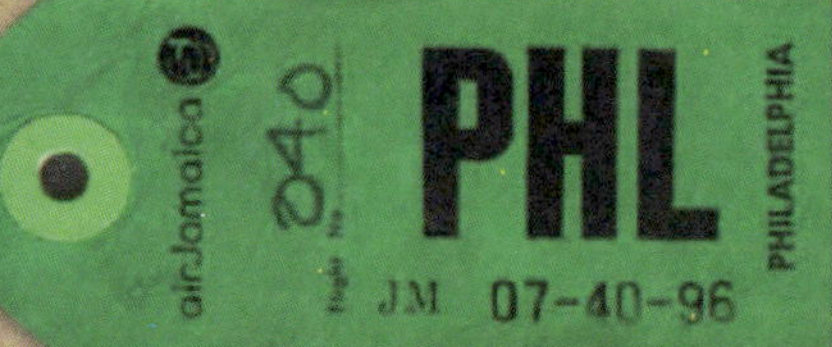
airJamaica
PHL
PHILADELPHIA
JM 07-40-96

ENCOURAGE LOCAL ENTERPRISE
TO RIDE WELL
Always Patronize BLUE BELL
Private Parties of every description catered for
LET US QUOTE YOU

Seat No.
INDIAN AIRLINES
KINDLY EMPLANE HERE

BOAC
CABIN BAGGAGE
IN PASSENGER'S
OWN CARE

CP Air
A
YYZ
TORONTO
38-31-53
Flight
60

A 2447
A. MEEK & SON
NAILBRIDGE
OUT

transair
YAM
SAULT STE. MARIE
52000

C5
10
225
STAMP
C5
10
225
STAMP

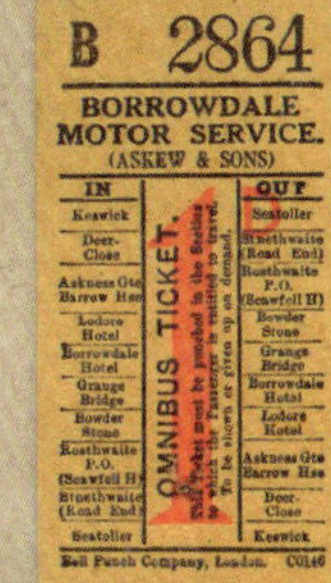
B 2864
BORROWDALE
MOTOR SERVICE.
(ASKEW & SONS)
IN
OUT
OMNIBUS TICKET.
Bell Punch Company, London.

IRAN AIR
FLIGHT
SEAT
IRAN AIR
BOARDING PASS
کارت عبور

Y 3234
RETURN
3d
OUT
SINGLE
IN

AVIANCA
LA LINEA AEREA COLOMBIANA
EQUIPAJE DE MANO
HAND-BAGGAGE

A 8738
THE SAFETY COACH
SERVICE, LTD.
(RED BAND BUS)
JERSEY, C. I.
9D
OMNIBUS TICKET

FARE PAID
CLASS
STAGE BOARDED
5D
ORD
31
LONDON
TRANSPORT
33226
ROUTE
TICKET No.
038
0040

Hotel
PRAHA
Belvedere
SOLO SUŠICE ČSN 494705

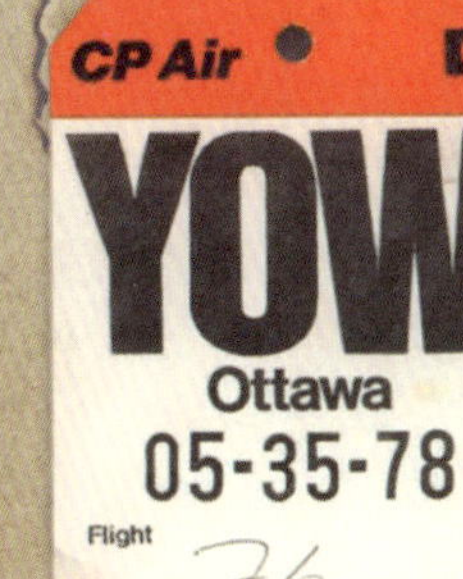
CP Air
YOW
Ottawa
05-35-78
Flight
76

EASTERN
PHL
PHILADELPHIA
PENNSYLVANIA
27-17-15

ARIANA AFGHAN AIRLINES
GROUP

C5
8
225
STAMP
C5
8
225
STAMP

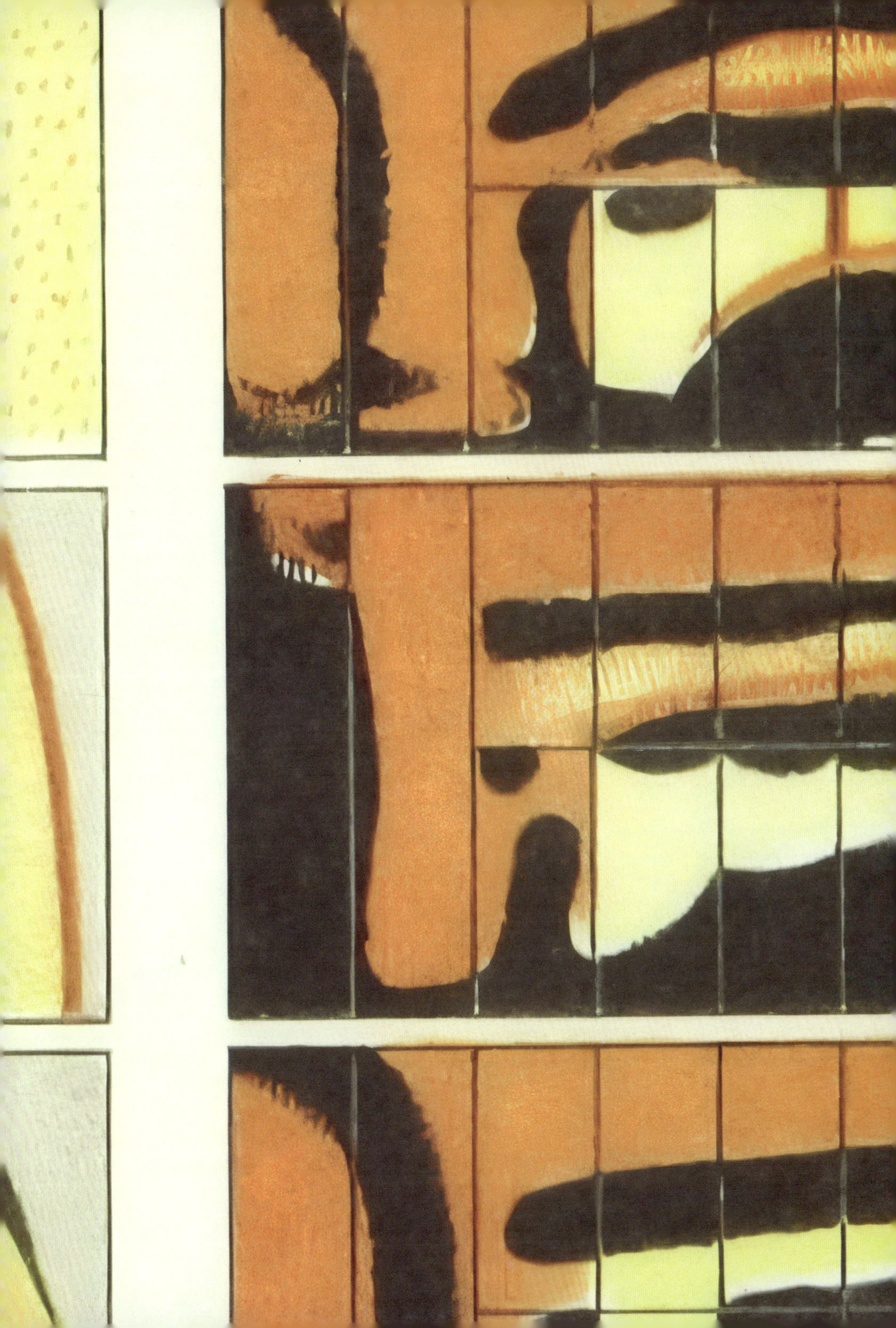

たてはちょう科（×1）

98．めすあかむらさき ♂

92．くじゃくちょう ♀

93．るりたては ♂

めすあかむらさき ♀

94．こひおどし ♂

99．やえやまむらさき ♂

95．たてはもどき ♀

21．みやまもんきちょう ♂

1

3

5

14

16

22

2

4

6

15

17

23

7

18

24

8

25

9

27

10

28

12

20

21

31

13

29

30

ARTIS DVORVM
ORBITA GLOBI TER
SOLSTI
BRV
DEL
ZVR.
Zodia
Arcticus
TEMPVS IX MENSIBVS RECVR
Cancri
AFRI
Æquinoctialis
ÆTHIOPICVS
opicus Capricorni
OCEANVS
SPATIO CIRCA
LVNA
SOLSTI

ALLO SOLEM CIRCVM
RESTRIS ANNVO.
TIVM
LVNA
Capricorni
RENS
CVRRIVS
VENVS
RECVRRENS
LVNA
MAR
DEL
ZVR.
MAR
Tropicus
DEL
Circulus
Zodia
C.A.
SOLEM CVRRENTIS
MARS
TIVM

WILLS'S CIGARETTES.
ARIES - THE RAM.

WILLS'S CIGARETTES.
SAGITTARIUS - THE ARCHER.

WILLS'S CIGARETTES.
LIBRA - THE BALANCE.

WILLS'S CIGARETTES.
SCORPIO - THE SCORPION.

WILLS'S CIGARETTES.
TAURUS - THE BULL.

WILLS'S CIGARETTES.
CAPRICORNUS - THE GOAT.

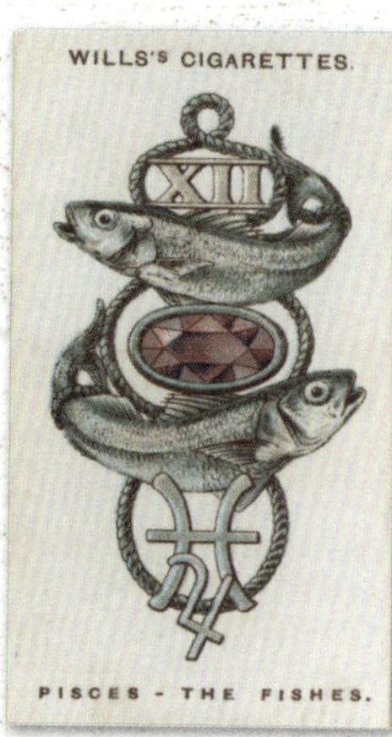
WILLS'S CIGARETTES.
PISCES - THE FISHES.

WILLS'S CIGARETTES.
LIBRA - THE BALANCE.

WILLS'S CIGARETTES.
VIRGO - THE VIRGIN.

WILLS'S CIGARETTES.
GEMINI - THE TWINS.

WILLS'S CIGARETTES.
CANCER - THE CRAB.

WILLS'S CIGARETTES.
LEO - THE LION.

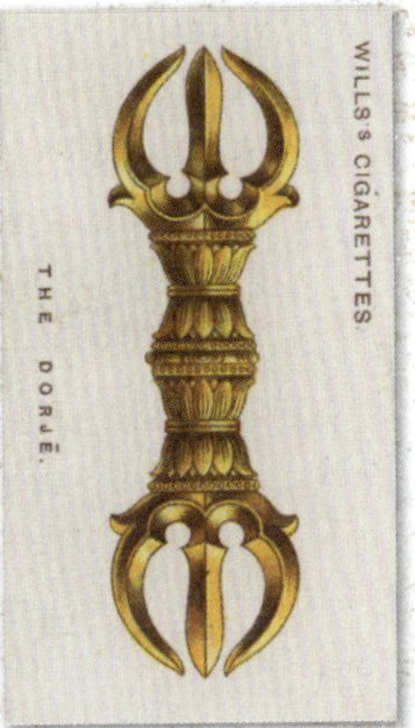
WILLS'S CIGARETTES.
THE DORJÉ.

WILLS'S CIGARETTES.
THE TORTOISE.

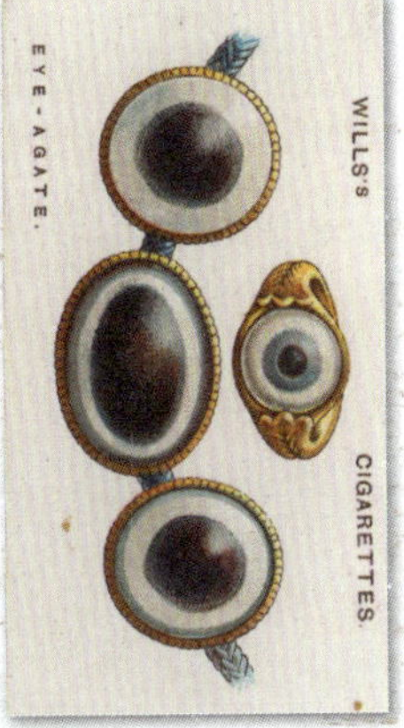
WILLS'S CIGARETTES.
EYE-AGATE.

WILLS'S CIGARETTES.
THE HEI-TIKI.

WILLS'S CIGARETTES.
GROTESQUE FIGURE.

WILLS'S CIGARETTES.
THE BULLA.

WILLS'S CIGARETTES.
THE TUSK.

WILLS'S CIGARETTES.
THE FISH.

WILLS'S CIGARETTES.
FOOD CHARM.

WILLS'S CIGARETTES.
ABRACADABRA
BRACADABR
RACADAB
ACADA
CAD
A
THE ABRACADABRA.

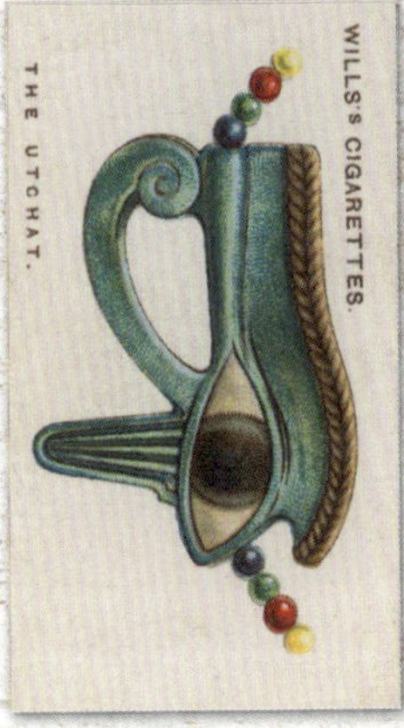
WILLS'S CIGARETTES.
THE UTCHAT.

WILLS'S CIGARETTES.
THE BUCKLE OF ISIS.

1er Avril.

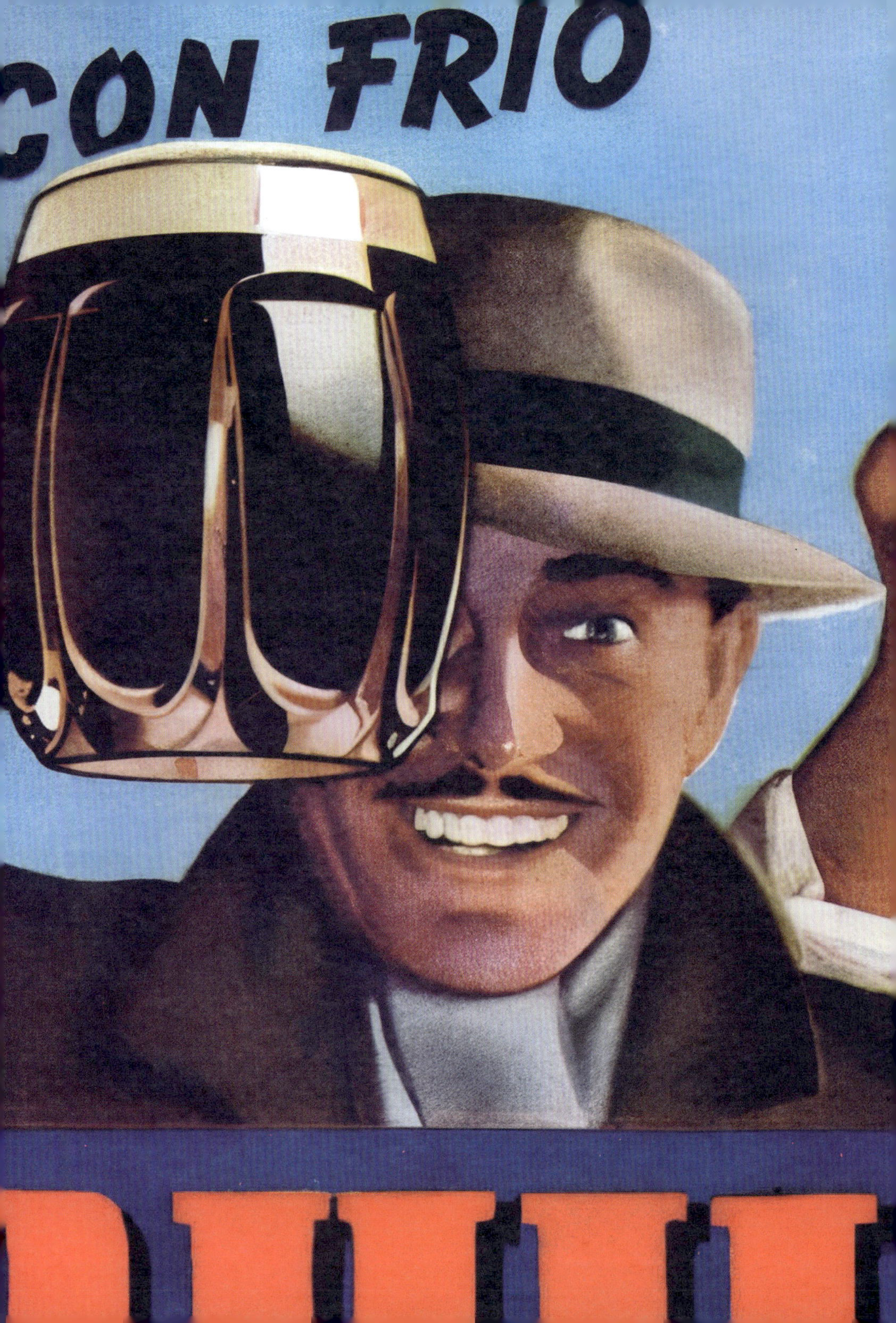
CON FRIO

CON CALOR

SAWTELL'S
Orade
KINGAROY

Wimmer's
ANYTHING
ARTIFICIALLY COLOURED & FLAVOURED
PRESERVATIVE ADDED
J. WIMMER · COOROY

F. WIMMER
AERATED WATER & CORDIAL MANUFACTURER
LEMONADE
QUALITY DRINKS
PHONE 32 NAMBOUR

MANUFACTURED AT THE
NORMAN FACTORY
BOWEN BRIDGE ROAD, BRISBANE
"NORMAN"
TOMATO SAUCE.

ARTIFICIALLY COLOURED
A PRODUCT OF THE ORANGE CRUSH CO.
KRINKLY
LIME FLAVOR
PRESERVATIVE ADDED
L. C. SAWTELL (Kingaroy) Pty. Ltd.

SUPERIOR
LA ROSA ESPAÑOLA
S. Y Cª
DE LA VUELTA ABAJO.

SAWTELL'S
S
750 ml
FLAVOURED
SYRUP
PRESERVATIVE ADDED
L. C. SAWTELL
(KINGAROY) PTY. LTD.

Fijne Koffie's
DE DRAAK
GENT
Tel:25.97.26

Eau-de-Vie-de-Cidre

SINCLAIR'S
CONDITION POWDERS.
For Horses, Cattle, Hogs and Sheep.
SAFE AND RELIABLE.

CITY'S
SUPERIOR
LEMONADE
City Bottling Coy.
DERRY.

SAWTELL'S
NEW
DRINK
COOLING & REFRESHING
KINGAROY

CHERRY-BRANDY
SURFIN

EUPENE'S
E
MONSA
S.B.C. and A.W.W.
WONDAI

ARTIFICIALLY COLOURED
SAWTELL'S
S&H
TRU-PASH
MADE FROM PASSION FRUIT & SUGAR
SAWTELL & MAURITZ
BRISBANE

'TRULEM'
Registered Trade Mark.
LEMON JUICE
CORDIAL
MADE FROM
BEST AUSTRALIAN LEMONS
AND FINE CANE SUGAR SYRUP
USE "TRULEM" INSTEAD OF
LEMONS FOR ALL DRINKS
PRESERVATISED
THIS FOOD CONTAINS NOT MORE THAN
2 GRAINS SULPHUR DIOXIDE PER PINT

MILLS BROTHER & CO.
Dealers in FOREIGN,
And Manufacturers of
Domestic Liquors,
BOURBON WHISKEY,
In Bond or Tax Paid,
104 Columbia Street,
Bet. Vine and Race,
CINCINNATI, O.

PHONE
W
84
PRESERVATIVE ADDED
LIME
ARTIFICIALLY
FLAVOUR
COLOURED
& SODA
J. WIMMER
AERATED WATER
MANUFACTURER
COOROY

WALLNUT KETCHUP
J. B. HAMBLEN & CO.
189 BROAD & 135 PURCHASE STS BOSTON

AERATED
"ORANA"
The Natural Flavour
of FRESHLY
SQUEEZED
ORANGES
ARTIFICIALLY COLOURED

120 AMORFOS, $75 + 5 SOC. SOC.
FOSFOREIRA PORTUGUESA, ESPINHO
bar

CURAÇAO
Surfin
Nº 959

SITREX
The best thirst Quencher
S
SAWTELL'S Brisbane

MADE BY NINOVE MATCH
PILULES DE SANTE
GEZONDHEIDSPILLEN
Pilules de Santé
DOCTEUR MANN
Dr MANN

JAVA
macaroni
MACARONI

CHERRY
BRANDY

Heno
PRAVIA

First published in the United Kingdom in 2025
by Skittledog, an imprint of Thames & Hudson Ltd,
6–24 Britannia Street, London WC1X 9JD

Designer: Alison Guile
Picture Research: Grace Wilmshurst
Production: Felicity Awdry

EU Authorized Representative: Interart S.A.R.L.
19 rue Charles Auray, 93500 Pantin, Paris, France
productsafety@thameshudson.co.uk
www.interart.fr

A CIP catalogue record for this book is available from the British Library

ISBN 978-1-83776-091-6
02

Printed and bound inn China by Win Choi Printing

Be the first to know about our new releases, exclusive content and author events by visiting:

thamesandhudson.com
thamesandhudsonusa.com
thamesandhudson.com.au